S0-BAJ-352

Party TIME!

Making Invitations, Favors, and Decorations

Martingale®
& COMPANY

Party Time! Making Invitations, Favors, and Decorations
© 2005 by Martingale & Company

Martingale & Company
20205 144th Avenue NE
Woodinville, WA 98072-8478 USA
www.martingale-pub.com

Printed in China
10 09 08 07   8 7 6 5 4

No part of this product may be reproduced in any form, unless otherwise stated, in which case reproduction is limited to the use of the purchaser. The written instructions, photographs, designs, projects, and patterns are intended for the personal, noncommercial use of the retail purchaser and are under federal copyright laws; they are not to be reproduced by any electronic, mechanical, or other means, including informational storage or retrieval systems, for commercial use. Permission is granted to photocopy patterns for the personal use of the retail purchaser.

The information in this book is presented in good faith, but no warranty is given nor results guaranteed. Since Martingale & Company has no control over choice of materials or procedures, the company assumes no responsibility for the use of this information.

Credits

President • Nancy J. Martin
CEO • Daniel J. Martin
VP and General Manager • Tom Wierzbicki
Publisher • Jane Hamada
Editorial Director • Mary V. Green
Managing Editor • Tina Cook
Technical Editor • Dawn Anderson
Copy Editor • Melissa Bryan
Design Director • Stan Green
Illustrator • Laurel Strand
Cover and Text Designer • Shelly Garrison
Photographers • Bill Lindner and Chris McArthur
Photo Assistant • Georgina Frankel
Photo Stylist • Susan Jorgensen

Library of Congress Cataloging-in-Publication Data

Party Time! Making Invitations, Favors, and Decorations
  p. cm.
 ISBN 978-1-56477-631-0
 1. Party decorations. 2. Holiday decorations.
 I. Martingale & Company.
 TT900.P3P37 2005
 745.594'1—dc22

       2005016001

Mission Statement

Dedicated to providing quality products and service to inspire creativity.

Contents

Introduction

The menu has been chosen. The guest list is set. The date is drawing near. Stories will be shared; spirits will be high. It's all coming together—the makings of a perfect party! Now it's time to add your creative touch and make that special occasion a one-of-a-kind experience for your guests.

Whether the gathering is simple or extravagant, all celebrations provide an opportunity to create cherished memories. Within the pages of this book, you'll discover quick and easy ways to dress up any event—and make it a day that your guests won't soon forget. With 15 party themes and more than 85 imaginative projects to choose from, you'll never run short on inspiration!

This unique collection features cheerful colors, rich textures, and unusual details that make each design stand out. Many projects lend themselves to assembly-line techniques, so you can reproduce a dozen or more of the same project in one sitting. Instructions feature straightforward how-tos, and several projects use ready-made materials for ultraquick results. Browse through the photos, choose a theme, and get ready to embellish your bash with sparkle and style.

Invitations

Invitations set the stage for your party. In addition to event details, you can quickly communicate an occasion, theme, or even a mood with the kind of invitation you send. You'll find lots of stylish choices throughout these pages,

4

including a patriotic flag invitation for a Fourth of July picnic, a graduation invitation that holds tiny pictures of the guest of honor, and even a house-warming invite embellished with a real metal key and paintbrush!

Decorations

Embellishing your everyday surroundings with decorations adds a magical touch to any party. From elegant to enchanting, the decorations within these pages will instantly infuse your celebration with festivity and warmth. Choose from centerpieces, napkin rings, coasters, an ice bucket, candle ornaments, and even whimsical pinwheels.

Favors

Favors provide a wonderful way to send your guests home with a memento of your time together. From chocolate-bar, potted-plant, and bath-salt favors to photo holders, party crackers, and wine-glass charms, these tiny keep-sakes let you give something back to those who attend your event. (As an alternative to the traditional bottle of wine, try using these favor ideas as simple, quick-to-make gifts to bring to the next party you are invited to!)

Whether for a holiday, a milestone, or just because, parties are a wonderful way to commemorate family, friends, and the highlights of our lives. So put a creative spin on your next event—and then get ready to party!

10... 9... 8... 7... 6...

Ring in the New Year!

December 31st

Festivities begin with dinner at Cafe Bella
6:30 pm

Cocktails and Champagne to follow
at the Hoenisch's
108 Old River Road

After the stroke of 12,
we'll welcome the new year with
ice skating by moonlight

New Year's Party Invitation

by Saralyn Ewald,
Sr. Designer, Archiver's

Print the invitation text onto patterned paper to fit within a 4" x 5" space. Trim the text block to size and adhere to shimmer paper. Trim the shimmer paper 1/8" from the edges on the sides and bottom and 3/4" from the edge at the top. Adhere the card to contrasting cardstock and trim 3/16" from the edges to create a border. Tear a corner piece from metallic paper and adhere to the center top of the card. Attach a clock charm.

Celebrate Coaster

by Saralyn Ewald,
Sr. Designer, Archiver's

Cut one circle each from shimmer paper and metallic paper to fit inside the rim of a glass coaster. Tear off one-third of the metallic circle and set the remainder aside. Adhere the torn paper to the shimmer paper, aligning the curved edges. Stamp *Celebrate* onto the metallic paper. Adhere the circle to the center of the coaster with liquid glue. Attach a clock charm. Punch stars from contrasting metallic paper and sprinkle onto the coaster. Fill the center of the coaster with Paper Glaze, thoroughly covering the decorative elements. Use the point of a pin to pop any air bubbles that may form. Allow the glaze to dry overnight.

New Year's Party Crackers

by Saralyn Ewald,
Sr. Designer, Archiver's

Cut a sheet of heavy cardstock in half both ways to make four 4¼" x 5½" rectangles. Cut one of the rectangles in half again to make two 2⅛" x 5½" rectangles. Roll each of the rectangles into a tube shape with a 4¼" circumference. Overlap the ends and secure with tape. Set two of the longer tubes aside. Trim a piece of mulberry paper to 9" x 12". Assemble and fill a party cracker following the manufacturer's instructions, using the long tube in the center of the mulberry paper and the shorter tubes on the ends. Wrap a scalloped note card around the center of the tube and secure in place. Trim patterned paper to 2" x 5", wrap the strip around the center of the tube, and secure.

Wine Glass Charm

*by Saralyn Ewald,
Sr. Designer, Archiver's*

Thread beads onto one half of an earring hoop. Open a jump ring with pliers and slide a celestial charm onto it. Close the jump ring and thread the ring onto the earring hoop. Continue adding beads to the hoop, leaving at least ⅛" of wire exposed at the end. Slide a crimp bead onto the end of the wire and use pliers to flatten the bead to prevent the other beads from falling off. Attach the hoop to the stem of the glass.

Ice Bucket

by Saralyn Ewald, Sr. Designer, Archiver's

Cut patterned paper into asymmetrical pieces. Adhere the pieces to the sides of a planter, using liquid glue. Use small pieces of paper to fill in the area around the claw feet. Allow to dry. Apply several coats of Mod Podge over the paper surface, allowing the surface to dry between coats.

arty Hat

by Dawn Anderson

Cut one hat piece from patterned paper, using the pattern on page 77. Roll the paper into a cone shape and secure with tape. Cut one piece each of patterned paper and cardstock and four pieces of mulberry paper to 1¾" x 12". Layer the papers and stitch together ⅛" from a long edge. Make cuts in the paper to the stitching line, spacing the cuts ⅛" apart, to make fringe. Crinkle the fringe between your fingers. Adhere the fringe to the inside edge of the hat with tape. Make additional fringe as necessary. Cut a 1½" length of fringe and roll it up along the stitching line to make a tassel. Insert the tassel into the top of the hat and adhere. Print the year onto patterned paper. Center a Page Pebble over the year and trim away excess paper. Adhere a circle sticker to a metal-rimmed tag and then adhere the year to the sticker. Attach the label to the hat. Install an eyelet on each side of the hat above the fringe. Secure a length of elastic cording to the eyelets.

Valentine's Day *Party*

Valentine Party Invitation
by Saralyn Ewald,
Sr. Designer, Archiver's

Trim cardstock to 5½" x 8½" and fold in half to make a 5½" x 4¼" card. Cut six 1⅜" squares from patterned papers and draw a border around the squares with a gold leafing pen. Adhere the squares to the front of the card at different angles, leaving ¼" to ½" between the squares. Thread a piece of metallic fiber through small buttons and secure in a knot on top. Adhere the buttons to the card. Print the invitation text onto patterned paper to fit in a 3¾" x 5" space. Cut the text block to size and adhere to the inside of the card, leaving an even border all around.

Decorative Charger Plate
by Saralyn Ewald,
Sr. Designer, Archiver's

Cut eight 2¾" x 12" strips from patterned papers. Cut the strips into triangle and wedge shapes, keeping half of the pieces 2¾" wide. Trim a portion off of some of the pieces for variety. Draw a border around each of the paper pieces with a gold leafing pen. Arrange the pieces to fit around the rim of a charger plate and glue in place, cutting the pieces to fit as needed. Color the outside and inside edge of the rim with the gold leafing pen. Cut a 7¼" circle from patterned paper and draw a border around the edge with the gold leafing pen. Adhere the circle to the center of the charger and allow the glue to dry. Apply an even coat of Mod Podge to the surface of the charger, allow to dry, and then apply a second coat.

Note: *Use this project as a decorative piece only. Because the materials used might not be food-safe, don't place food directly on the surface of the charger.*

Pinstripe Favor Box
by Dawn Anderson

Print text onto cardstock. Center a Page Pebble over the text and adhere. Trim away the excess cardstock. Insert the Page Pebble into a coin mount. Join two jump rings and attach one to the loop of the coin mount. Wrap a length of ribbon around a small box filled with party favors, inserting one end through the other jump ring. Tie a bow.

Heart Soap Favor

by Dawn Anderson

Trim a piece of patterned paper to fit over the outer sleeve of a slider box and adhere in place. Trim a piece of patterned paper to wrap around the box insert, allowing an extra ½" to wrap to the inside of the box. Adhere in place. Adhere ribbon around the outer sleeve of the box. Position a Poemstone onto cardstock and trim around the edges, leaving a contrasting border. Secure the Poemstone to the box sleeve. Attach a thank-you tag to a lacy heart charm and secure them to the center of the box sleeve, overlapping the Poemstone. Place tissue paper and heart soap in the box insert and slide into the outer sleeve.

Valentine's Party!

When: February 14, 2006
Where: The Anderson's
Time: 6:00 pm
R.S.V.P: February 5, 2006

Heart Charm Invitation
by Dawn Anderson

Print the invitation text onto patterned paper to fit within a 5½" x 4" space and trim the text block to size. Tear a contrasting piece of patterned paper across a corner and adhere to the corner of the text block, aligning the edges. Trim the cardstock to 6" x 4½". Center the text block on the cardstock and adhere. Make a loop in the end of a 3" length of wire, using round-nose pliers. Thread a bead onto the opposite end of the wire. Trim the wire to ⅜" and make another loop in the end. Hang one loop from a spiral clip. Attach a heart charm to the other loop, using chain-nose pliers to open the loop. Tie a length of ribbon to the left side of the clip and position the clip on the card. Print text for the tag onto patterned paper and trim to size. Insert the text block into the clip.

Valentine Cone Favor
by Saralyn Ewald, Sr. Designer, Archiver's

Cut a cone piece from cardstock, using the cone favor pattern on page 78. Adhere the piece to the wrong side of patterned paper with liquid glue and let dry. Trim away excess paper around the cardstock piece. Draw a border around the patterned side of the cone piece, using a gold leafing pen. Roll the paper into a cone shape and secure with tape. Thread metallic fiber through the holes of small buttons and tie knots on the tops. Secure the buttons along the straight edge of the cone. Using the straight edge as the center, punch holes on each side of the cone about ½" from the upper edge. Cut an 11" piece of ribbon and thread the ends through the holes from the inside. Knot the ends, leaving tails.

Easter Celebration

Mark your next Easter celebration with egg and bunny motifs in pretty pastels.

Easter Invitation
by Dawn Anderson

Trim cardstock to 5½" x 8½" and fold in half to make a 5½" x 4¼" card. Trim patterned paper to 5½" x 5¾" and adhere to the card, folding the excess to the back. Photocopy a bunny image onto cardstock, resizing as necessary, and trim the photocopy to 5½" x 3". Apply glitter glue underneath the bunny, let dry, and adhere to the card. Adhere trim to the lower edge of the bunny paper. Print text onto patterned paper and cut to fit inside a page tab and a metal art tag. Cut a scant ⅜" slit in the card along the top edge of the cardstock on the right side. Attach ribbon to the tab and insert the tab into the slit. Glue sequins to the lower portion of the card.

Easter Basket Favor
by Dawn Anderson

Paint the inside and rim of an oval box. Photocopy a bunny image onto cardstock, resizing as necessary. Apply glitter glue underneath the bunny and let dry. Trim the cardstock, centering the bunny, to cover the outside of the box, and adhere in place. Cut a ⅜" strip of cardstock for the handle and adhere a strip of trim down the center. Secure the handle to the inside of the box to make a basket. Adhere trim to the top edge of the basket. Rub paint into the grooves of a Charmed Word and wipe off the excess. Print text onto patterned paper and adhere the Charmed Word above the text. Trim to size to make a tag. Adhere to cardstock and trim ⅛" from the edges. Attach an eyelet in the tag and secure the tag to the handle of the basket with ribbon.

Glittered Egg Vase
by Dawn Anderson

Glue a candle cup to the center of a wood disk. Using an X-Acto knife, trim the top off a papier-mâché egg in a zigzag pattern. Seal the egg inside and out. Glue the bottom of the egg to the top of the candle cup. Apply two coats of paint to the egg, inside and out. Apply two coats of paint to the wood base. Sand the base lightly to expose the wood in some areas. Apply varnish to the base and to the inside of the egg. Paint dots on the egg. Apply clear adhesive to half of the egg and sprinkle with Glamour Dust. Repeat on the other half. Print text centered on cardstock and trim to 8¼" x 1". Cut a V shape from each end. Adhere the label to contrasting cardstock and trim ⅛" from the edges. Lightly fold a tuck in the label on each side of the text. Adhere the label to the egg. Place a vase inside, securing it with floral clay.

Easter Egg Place Cards

by Dave Brethauer

Cut strips at least 1⅝" wide from note cards. Punch an egg shape at the center of the lower edge of each card strip. Glue a piece of 1½"-wide ribbon behind the opening. Cut a length of ⅛"-wide ribbon and glue it from the top of the egg to the top edge of the card. Print guests' names onto cardstock. Trim close to the name and clip the corners at the left edge to create a tag shape. Adhere the name tag to the place card where the ribbon meets the egg.

Fourth of July *Picnic*

Patriotic stars and stripes set the scene for the perfect picnic party.

*F*lag Invitation
by Genevieve A. Sterbenz

Adhere a flag to the front of a tag. Punch 10 stars from cardstock and adhere above and below the flag. Stamp the text onto the flag and emboss the stamped impression with embossing powder and a heat tool. Cut four flags from a banner of flags, adhere to cardstock, and trim ⅛" from the edges. Adhere the flags in a column along the left side of another tag. Next to each flag, write the date, time, place, and any other necessary information. Tie the two tags together with ribbon.

*S*tar Luminary
by Genevieve A. Sterbenz

Using the star luminary template listed on page 68, cut the small inner star from the template. Trace the small star template onto a Wallies flag, cut it out, and set aside. Trace the large star outline from the star luminary template onto cardstock; lift the template at the lower edge and use the template markings as a guide to draw in the bottom two star points. Cut out the cardstock star, and set aside. Trace the star luminary template onto patterned paper, and cut on the marked lines. Adhere the cardstock star to the patterned star luminary cutout over the star portion of the design, keeping the edges aligned. Adhere the star cut from the flag to the center of the cardstock star. Using the star luminary template as a guide, fold the design in half vertically and then unfold. Fold back flaps A and B and secure where the flaps meet. Place the completed design in front of a votive holder, such as the red beaded one shown opposite.

*F*lag Garland
by Genevieve A. Sterbenz

Cut four 3½" squares from cardstock and set aside. Trace a star template onto two Wallies flags, cut out, and set aside. On a flat work surface, place the following items, face down in a row, leaving 1" between each item: flag, cardstock square, flag, cardstock square flag. Lay gold cording across the items, ¼" from the top edges. Apply spray adhesive to three more flags and the remaining cardstock squares. Adhere the flags and squares to the matching pieces, trapping the cording between the layers. Be sure to keep the edges even and maintain the spacing between the pieces. Adhere the two stars cut from flags to the centers of the cardstock squares to complete the garland.

Fourth of July Favor Basket
by Dawn Anderson

Adhere ribbon around the middle of a nut-cup basket. Attach a star eyelet to the front of the basket over the ribbon. Print the guest's name onto cardstock and trim to size. Adhere the name block to contrasting cardstock and trim ⅛" from the edges to create a border. Attach an eyelet to the left side of the name tag. Thread cording through the eyelet and tie the tag to the basket handle.

Celebrate Independence Day!

This seed packet contains red, white and blue wildflowers.

Scatter the red poppy, annual baby's breath and blue cornflower seeds to create your American flag garden.

Seed-Packet Favor
by Dawn Anderson

Adhere a flag seed packet to patterned paper and trim ⅜" from the edges of the packet to create a border. Print text onto cardstock to fit in a 1¾" x 3¼" space. Cut the cardstock to size and trim across the top corners to make a tag shape. Adhere the tag to patterned paper and trim ⅛" from the edges. Adhere the tag to the center of the seed packet paper, aligning the upper edges. Punch a ⅛" hole at the center of the tag through all layers, a scant ⅜" from the upper edge, being careful not to cut into the seed packet. Tie ribbon through the hole and attach a decorative brad.

Pinwheel

by Genevieve A. Sterbenz

Cut a 7" square from solid paper and another from patterned paper. Adhere the papers wrong sides together, using spray adhesive. With the solid paper facing up, fold the square diagonally in half, matching the corners, and crease a line. Unfold and repeat with the remaining corners. Using a pencil, make a mark on each creased line 1¾" from the center point. Cut along the lines from each corner to the marked points. Bring one corner to the center of the square. Repeat with alternating corners and insert a pushpin through all four points into the center of the paper. Secure the pinwheel to a block of Styrofoam. Punch 35 stars from cardstock and adhere the stars to the solid arms of the pinwheel. Remove the pinwheel from the Styrofoam, place one or two seed beads onto the pushpin, and insert the pin into a wood dowel about 1" from the end.

Halloween Party

Date: October 31, 2006

Time: 6:00 pm

Place: The Andersons

RSVP: October 25, 2006

Thanks

Halloween *Party*

No tricks here—just whimsical treats for a chic haunted hangout.

*H*alloween Party Invitation
by Dawn Anderson

Trim cardstock to 11" x 7⅞" and fold in half to make a 5½" x 7⅞" card. Cut a 5" x 2⅜" rectangle and a 5" square from coordinating patterned papers. Adhere the patterned papers to the front of the card and cover the join with ribbon. Attach photo anchors with brads. Create a message with alphabet stickers. Print the party information on 7gypsies paper, trim to size, adhere to a negative strip, and secure to the card.

*S*keleton Thank-You Card
by Dawn Anderson

Trim cardstock to 8½" x 5½" and fold in half to make a 4¼" x 5½" card. Cut a 3¾" x 3⅜" rectangle and a 3¾" x 1⅝" rectangle from coordinating patterned papers. Adhere the patterned papers to the front of the card and cover the join with ribbon. Create a message with alphabet stickers. Trim 7gypsies paper to size, adhere to a negative strip, and secure to the card. Attach a skeleton charm.

*H*alloween Pinwheel
by Genevieve A. Sterbenz

Paint a wood dowel and set aside. Cut a 7" square from patterned paper and another from textured paper. Adhere the papers wrong sides together using spray adhesive. With the textured paper facing up, fold the square diagonally in half, matching the corners, and crease a line. Unfold and repeat with the remaining corners. Using a pencil, make a mark on each creased line 1¾" from the center point. Cut along the lines from each corner to the marked points. Bring one corner to the center of the square. Repeat with alternative corners and insert a pushpin through all four points into the center of the paper. Secure the pinwheel to a block of Styrofoam. Punch 35 circles from glossy solid paper and adhere the circles to the textured arms of the pinwheel. Remove the pinwheel from the Styrofoam, place one or two seed beads onto the pushpin, and insert the pin into the dowel about 1" from the end.

Halloween Favor Basket
by Dawn Anderson

Print the guest's name onto patterned paper and trim to size. Adhere the name block to cardstock and trim ⅛" from the edges to create a border. Adhere the name tag to the handle of a nut-cup basket, centering the tag at the top of the handle. Using a needle and thread, sew a bat button to the basket handle at the top of the name tag.

Wine Glass Charms
by Dawn Anderson

Cut a piece of wire 3½" long. Make a double loop at one end of the wire with round-nose pliers. Thread beads onto the wire for about 2¾". Make a double loop in the wire at the remaining end and trim off the excess. Open a jump ring with chain-nose pliers. Place the loop of a Halloween charm onto the jump ring. Attach the jump ring to the center of the beaded wire and close the jump ring. Bend the beaded wire into a circle. Attach the beaded circle to the stem of the glass.

Popcorn Box
by Dawn Anderson

Trim paper to cover each side of a popcorn box, trimming along the top scalloped edge and allowing ¼" extra on one long edge for the underlap. Adhere the paper lightly to the front of the box, wrapping the excess around the side edge. Adhere the paper to the side of the box in the same manner, covering the overlap. Repeat around the box, lifting the paper on the front edge to wrap the excess paper from the adjacent side. Smooth the paper in place. Tie ribbon through the hole in a metal-rimmed tag, add a chipboard word to the center, and adhere to the front of the box.

Thanksgiving Dinner *Party*

Dim the lights at the dinner table and let these bead-and-brass decorations sparkle.

*T*hanksgiving Invitation
by Christine Falk

Print *ive Thanks* onto parchment cardstock just below the center of the paper. Fold the parchment in half so the text falls just beyond the fold. Trim to 5" x 7", centering the text and allowing 1⅝" at the beginning of the message for the G. Print the letter G onto parchment cardstock, cut out, and set aside. Print a message onto cardstock, for example, the definition of Thanksgiving or a poem or blessing. Trim the cardstock and vellum to 3" x 7", allowing space for a window above the text. Use vellum tape to secure the cardstock to the vellum. Punch a 1¾" square into the papers above the message. Cut a 2½" square from metallic paper and adhere to the back of the opening. Adhere the layered papers to the card. Punch a 1½" square in the center of the metallic square. Adhere the 1½" metallic square at bottom left of the card and adhere the G over the top. String beads onto gold thread and tie knots after each group of five beads. Tie the thread around the fold of the card. Attach a skeleton leaf inside the window opening.

*M*esh Votive Favor
by Christine Falk

Cut brass mesh to fit around a votive holder, positioning the mesh just under the top lip of the holder, and adding ½" to both the length and width for the hems. Lightly mark lines ¼" from all edges of the mesh. Align a ruler with the markings and fold up the edges, creasing lightly. Crease hems firmly with the edge of the ruler. Apply tacky tape to the outside of the hems. Wrap the mesh around the votive, starting at one corner. Adhere metallic trim around the lip of the votive holder, overlapping the mesh slightly. Lightly apply Rub 'n Buff to a small brass frame using a rag. Print a monogram initial onto cardstock, cut to fit inside the frame, and secure to the votive holder.

*B*eaded Napkin Ring and Place Card
by Christine Falk

Wrap 24-gauge wire around a paper-towel tube 10 times; add 2" and then trim. Make a couple of tight loops at the end to prevent beads from slipping off. String beads onto the wire and secure with tight loops at the opposite end. Wrap the wire around the tube and hold in place with tape. Cut a 12" length of wire and thread through the eye of an embroidery needle. Weave the wire over and under the rows of beads until you get to the edge, and then weave it back. Twist the wire ends together and trim to ⅜". Repeat the weaving process in two more locations around the tube. Remove the tube and press the wire ends to the inside of the napkin ring. Glue a leaf charm in place. Attach a spiral clip to the beaded wire on one side of the leaf. Print the guest's name onto cardstock, trim to size for a place card, and insert into the spiral clip.

Celebrate friends, family &
all we have to be thankful for!

Join us on November 24th
for good food and great company.

3:00 pm
at Kevin & Alanna's House

2416 Oak Street South
Saint Paul

Please bring a dish to share.

Give us a call if you will not be able to come.

Favor Box
by Dawn Anderson

Rub paint over an unassembled favor box and lid in a swirling pattern, using a rag. When dry, fold together the box and lid. Wrap ribbon around favor-filled box and secure the ends through a ribbon charm. Print a name onto cardstock and trim to size. Apply ink to the outer edges of the name tag and attach it under the ribbon.

Leaf Invitation
by Saralyn Ewald,
Sr. Designer, Archiver's

Print the invitation text onto cardstock, starting 1½" from the top, and trim to size. Cut a contrasting piece of cardstock ⅜" larger all around. Center the text block onto the contrasting cardstock and adhere along the upper edge. Attach a die-cut leaf to the card. Punch two holes in the leaf about ½" apart and tie raffia through the holes.

A

by Saralyn Ewald,
Sr. Designer, Archiver's

Score and lightly fold some of the maple
leaves and green leaves down the center.
Position and glue the 45 maple leaves
around a grapevine wreath to cover the
wreath base. Glue six to seven green leaves
around the wreath near the center. Glue the
additional leaves to the wreath, striving
for an even arrangement of
colors and shapes.

Christmas *Party*

Invoke the holiday spirit with simple ways to make your guests feel special.

*T*ree Invitation
by Dave Brethauer

Stamp a tall triangle shape onto cardstock. Stamp a pine tree design over the triangle. Trim the cardstock to 1¼" x 3". Trim contrasting cardstock to 1⅜" x 3⅛" and adhere the piece, centered, to the back of the stamped-tree cardstock. Trim patterned paper to 5⅜" x 4⅛" and adhere to the front of a note card. Adhere the stamped image to the card. Dot the tree with clear glitter glue and sprinkle with glitter.

*C*hocolate Bar Favor
by Dave Brethauer

Stamp a small triangle shape four times onto cardstock, leaving enough space between the triangles to accommodate a second row of triangles. Using a slightly different shade of ink, stamp the small triangle again five times across the cardstock, slightly higher than the previous row. Stamp a pine tree design over each triangle. Trim the stamped cardstock to 2" x 5¼". Trim contrasting cardstock papers to 2⅛" x 5⅜" and 2½" x 5½". Adhere the paper layers together and attach to the center of a slim tag. Adhere a wrapped chocolate bar inside the tag.

*O*rnament Place Cards
by Dave Brethauer

Cut strips at least 1⅝" wide from note cards. Punch a 1¼" circle at the center of the lower edge of each card strip. Glue a piece of ribbon behind the opening. Cut a length of cording and glue it from the top of the circle to the top edge of the card. Print guests' names onto cardstock. Trim close to the name and clip the corners at the left edge to create a tag shape. Adhere the name tag to the place card where the cording meets the circle.

Snowflake Thank-You Card
by Savvy Stamps

Stamp a solid circle in the center of a metal-rimmed tag. Stamp a snowflake design over the circle. Tie ribbon at the top of the tag. Adhere the tag to a note card and stamp *thank you* on the card.

Glittered Pinecone Boxes
by Dawn Anderson

Paint the inside and outside of a pinecone-shaped papier-mâché box. Apply glue to the outside of one box piece and sprinkle with Glamour Dust. Repeat for the other half of the box. Apply paint to the grooves of a mini tag and wipe off the excess. Slide the tag onto the gold string of the box.

JOIN US
To Celebrate
Ali's 8th Birthday

many thanks

THANKS FOR COMING MEGAN!

Birthday *Party*

These easy, elegant designs will make everyone feel like the guest of honor!

*B*irthday Invitation
by Savvy Stamps

Print the invitation text onto the bottom of three sheets of coordinating cardstock. Trim the top layer of paper to 3⅞" x 6¼", the middle to 3⅞" x 6¾", and the bottom to 3⅞" x 8¼", centering the text across the width. Score a line 1" from the upper edge of the bottom layer of paper and fold the flap to the front. Layer the papers, aligning the top edges at the fold, and punch two holes ½" apart in the center of the flap. Tie ribbon through the holes. Stamp a large circle on the card and stamp a cake design in the center of it. Apply rubber cement to the image and sprinkle with glitter.

*F*avor Packet
by Savvy Stamps

Trim cardstock to 8½" x 8½". Fold up at 2½" and again at 3½" from the first fold, and set aside. Print text onto contrasting cardstock and trim to 8½" x 2¼". Stamp circles across the strip. Center the strip over the folded cardstock, with the flaps at the back. Fold a ribbon in half and place over the layered papers at the center of the left edge. Stitch ½" from the edge, catching the ribbon in the stitching. Fill the packet with treats and stitch the remaining end closed.

*C*ake Thank-You Card
by Savvy Stamps

Stamp a metal-rimmed tag with a solid circle block, and then with a cake slice design. Glue a paper flower to the top of the cake slice. Tie a ribbon through the hole in the tag. Adhere the tag to a note card and stamp *many thanks* on the card.

Heather's turning 30!

Please come to a surprise
birthday party!

Date: June 26, 2007
Time: 1:00 pm
Place: Sydney's in Edina
RSVP: June 16, 2007

Birthday Invitation
by Dawn Anderson

Print the invitation text onto cardstock to fit within a 3" x 6½" space, allowing room for the stamped image. Stamp a flower onto cardstock. Apply glue to the flower petals and sprinkle with Glamour Dust. Trim the flower to size. Trim vellum ⅛" larger than the flower on all sides, cover vellum with glue, and sprinkle with Glamour Dust. Adhere the flower to the glittered vellum and attach to the card. Cut patterned paper to 3¾" x 7¼". Center the card front over the patterned paper and punch a hole in the papers about ¾" from the top. Fold ribbon in half and insert the folded end through the hole. Attach a coordinating snap over the hole, securing the ribbon in place.

Favor Gift Box
by Dawn Anderson

Wrap ribbon twice around the center of a treat-filled box and secure the ends on top of the box. Adhere a fabric letter to cardstock and trim ³/₁₆" from the edges. Adhere the letter to the top of the box.

A unique favor and centerpiece spotlight tiny photos of the proud graduate.

Graduation Invitation
by Saralyn Ewald,
Sr. Designer, Archiver's

Print the invitation text onto cardstock, starting 1¼" below the top edge, and allowing 1¼" after the first line for rub-on letters. Apply rub-on text and trim the text block to size. Apply ink to the edges of the text block, adhere to patterned paper, and trim ¼" from the edges. Wrap wire around a marker to create loops, and then pull the loops apart slightly and flatten. Use round-nose pliers to make a loop in each end of the flattened wire. Coil the wire around the loops to make ½"-diameter coils. Position the wire across the card and fold the coiled ends to the back. Insert small photos into the wire coils, securing with glue dots.

Wire Photo Holder Favor and Thank-You Note
by Saralyn Ewald,
Sr. Designer, Archiver's

Print text onto cardstock to fit within a 3½" x 5" space, allowing room at the top and bottom for the photo and wire holder. Apply ink to the edges of the text block, adhere to patterned paper, and trim ¼" from the edges. Cut a 5" length of wire and make a loop at one end, using round-nose pliers. Wrap the wire around the loop to make a coil, attach the coil to the card, and insert a photo. Cut a 25" length of wire and make a loop at each end. Wrap the wire around each loop to make coils 1" in diameter. Bend the wire in half, bringing the coils together. Pull the coils slightly out to the sides to make a V, and then fold the wire ends in, about 2" from each coil, so the coils meet at the center with the remaining wire forming a triangle. Slip the thank-you card into the coils to stand it up.

Floral Centerpiece with Photos
by Saralyn Ewald,
Sr. Designer, Archiver's

Cut a 40" length of wire and make a loop at each end, using round-nose pliers. Wrap the wire around each loop to make coils ⅝" in diameter. Starting about 4" from one end, wrap the wire several times around the neck of a vase. When you have about 4" remaining at the opposite end, wrap one end of the wire around the other end a couple times to secure, and then pull the ends apart. Insert photos into the wire coils.

THANK YOU VERY MUCH

Graduation Favor Bag
by Saralyn Ewald, Sr. Designer, Archiver's

Cut the two-piece graduation cap from cardstock, using the patterns on page 78. Adhere the hat pieces together, aligning the front edge of the top piece with the dashed line on the bottom piece. Install a brad at the marked point. Punch a hole in one side of the hat. Stamp text onto cardstock and trim to size. Adhere the text block to contrasting cardstock and trim 1/8" from the edges. Punch a hole in the tag. Cut 3/16" strips from cardstock and run the strips through a paper crimper. Place candy and crimped paper into a cellophane treat bag. Turn down the top 1" of the bag twice. Punch two holes in the center of the folded cellophane. Tie curling ribbon through the holes of the bag, hat, and tag.

*F*avor Tin
by Dawn Anderson

Print the names of various nuts onto patterned paper and set aside. Cut a strip of contrasting patterned paper to fit around a circular tin, allowing for ¼" of overlap at the ends. From the paper printed with nut names, cut a strip ¼" narrower than the patterned paper and adhere together, leaving a border on the long edges. Adhere the layered paper strip to the outside of the tin. Cut a circle of patterned paper to fit inside the rim of the lid. Cut a circle of nut paper ¼" smaller in diameter. Adhere the circles together and secure to the lid. Wrap ribbon around the center of the tin, taping the ends in place on the bottom. Print text onto cardstock for the label and trim to fit inside a small metal frame. Attach the frame to the center of the lid.

love blooms

Shower our bride-to-be Kathleen
with well wishes!

Join us on Saturday, August 8th
at 1:00 pm

2416 Oak Street South
Saint Paul

Please r.s.v.p. Megan at (615) 345 - 7654

love
blooms

Thank you for joining us

Bridal *Shower*

Choose from two themes—cheerful flowers or dainty fashion accessories.

Flower Invitation

by Saralyn Ewald,
Sr. Designer, Archiver's

Brush paint over a decorative metal brad, allowing the metal to show through. Print the invitation text onto cardstock to fit in a 4½" x 6½" space, allowing 1⅜" at the top and 2" of space at the center. Stamp *love blooms* at the top of the text block. Adhere the text block to cardstock and trim ¼" from the edges. Cut a 1¼" x 12" band from patterned paper and a 1" x 4" rectangle from cardstock. Adhere the cardstock to the center back of the band to raise it from the invitation and give dimension. Secure the band around the center of the card. Punch a hole in the center of a decorative flower and install the brad. Adhere the flower to the band.

Favor Bag

by Saralyn Ewald,
Sr. Designer, Archiver's

Brush paint over a decorative metal brad, allowing the metal to show through. Print text onto cardstock to fit in a 4½" x 1½" space, allowing 1⅛" at the top and 1¾" on the left side. Stamp "love blooms" at the top, starting 1¾" from the left edge. Trim cardstock to 5" x 4" and fold in half to make a 5" x 2" card. Adhere the text block to the center front of the card. Punch a hole in the center of a decorative flower and install the brad. Adhere the flower to the card. Fill a glassine envelope with almonds, close the envelope flap, and secure with tape. Adhere the top of the envelope to the inside back of the card. Apply adhesive dots across the front of the envelope and press the card front in place.

Utensil Bucket

by Saralyn Ewald,
Sr. Designer, Archiver's

Brush paint over decorative metal brads, allowing the metal to show through. Tear patterned paper into pieces about ½" x 3", keeping the pattern running in the same direction. Using liquid glue, adhere the paper pieces vertically to a galvanized metal bucket, one piece at a time, until the entire bucket is covered. Allow to dry thoroughly. Apply a coat of Mod Podge over the paper, allow to dry, and then apply a second coat. Punch a hole in the center of decorative flowers and install a brad in each hole. Adhere the flowers to the outer rim of the bucket along the upper edge.

Bridal Shower Invitation
by Dawn Anderson

Trim textured cardstock to 11¼" x 7⅜" and fold in half to make a 5⅝" x 7⅜" card. Trim a piece of cardstock to 4⅜" x 6⅛" and adhere to the center of the card. Trim patterned paper to 4⅛" x 5⅞", apply ink to the edges, and adhere to the card. Stamp a dress image onto cardstock and cut out, adding tabs to the shoulders. Apply glue over the dress and sprinkle with Glamour Dust. Glue sequins to the dress. Attach cording and a tiny paper flower to the waistline. Attach the dress to a metal hanger, folding the shoulder tabs to the back. Adhere the dress to the card. Stamp text onto cardstock and trim to 5⅝" x ⅜". Apply ink to the edges and adhere to the bottom of the card. Attach a swirl clip to the lower-right edge.

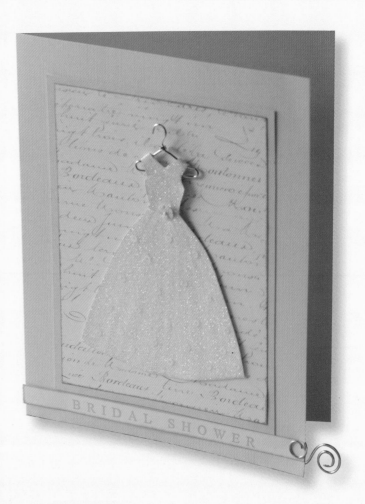

Potpourri Favor Box
by Dawn Anderson

Place potpourri beads in a round acrylic box. Print text onto cardstock and trim to fit behind a frame-shaped metal label. Adhere in place. Thread lengths of ribbon through the ends of the label. Center the label on the front of the container, wrap the ribbon around to the back, and tape the ends in place. Cover the ends with a sticker.

Purse Favor
by Dawn Anderson

Fill a clear vinyl purse with mints. Tie ribbon around the purse. Twist the stems of three velvet flowers together and secure under ribbon. Print the guest's name onto cardstock and trim to size. Adhere the name to textured cardstock and trim a scant ⅛" from the edges. Repeat with another color of cardstock, trimming ⅛" from the edges. Place the card between the purse handles.

Please join us in the
celebration of our love

Kathleen M. Bauer
and
Mark J. Wagner

Saturday, June 2, 2006
5 o'clock p.m.

Saint Mark's Church
Davenport, Iowa

Reception to follow
Ripple Creek Arboretum

May each bloom
blossom this new love.

Kathleen and Mark
June 2, 2006

Wedding Celebration

Tiny floral embellishments make these designs perfect for a garden wedding.

Wedding Invitation

by Saralyn Ewald,
Sr. Designer, Archiver's

Punch flowers from cardstock and glue a rhinestone to the center of each. Print the invitation text onto vellum to fit in a 4" x 6¼" space. Trim ribbed paper to 4¼" x 6½". Adhere the top edges of the vellum and ribbed paper together, using vellum tape. Adhere the back of the layered papers to patterned paper and trim ⅜" from the edges. Glue the punched flowers over the top edges of the vellum and ribbed papers.

Flower-Seed Favor

by Saralyn Ewald,
Sr. Designer, Archiver's

Punch flowers from cardstock and glue a rhinestone to the center of each. Print the tag text onto vellum to fit in a 2¼" x 2⅜" space. Trim patterned paper to 2⅜" x 2½". Adhere the top edges of the vellum and patterned paper together, using vellum tape. Cut a 2¾" x 3¾" rectangle from ribbed paper and trim the corners off one short end to make a tag. Adhere the layered papers to the tag. Glue the punched flowers over the top edges of the vellum and ribbed papers. Punch a hole in the tag, tie ribbon through it, and use double-sided adhesive to attach the tag to a packet of flower seeds.

Candle Decoration

by Saralyn Ewald,
Sr. Designer, Archiver's

Paint wood letters to spell *LOVE*. Cover the sides of a square box with patterned paper, securing with liquid glue and allowing for ¼" to be folded to the inside. Glue the letters to the box and turn the box so the letters face up until dry. Cut pieces of floral foam to fit inside the box, and secure with hot glue. Vary the height of the foam pieces so the candles will sit at three different levels. Set pillar candles inside glass candle holders and place in the box. Cover any visible foam with moss. Set the box on a coordinating cake stand. Insert an artificial rose and rosebud into the floral foam around the candles, and arrange a rose and bud on the cake stand around the box.

May each bloom
celebrate this new love.

Kathleen and Mark
June 2, 2006

Cathie & Dave

love \lŭv\ n : a deep, tender, ineffable feeling of affection and solicitude toward a person

Wedding Rings Invitation
by Christine Falk

Print the couple's names onto cardstock just below the center of the paper and fold the paper in half. Trim to 5" x 7", centering the text. Print a definition of love onto cardstock. Trim the cardstock and patterned vellum to 3" x 7", allowing space for a window above the text. Secure the cardstock to the vellum. Punch a 1¾" square into the layered papers above the definition. Cut a 2½" square from metallic paper and adhere to the back of the window. Adhere the layered papers to the card. Punch a 1½" square in the center of the metallic square. Tie ribbon around the fold of the card. Tie ribbon around two craft wedding rings and secure to the card so that they are visible through the window.

Candle Favor
by Dawn Anderson

Wrap a glass candle box with ribbon and tape the ends in place on the top of the lid. Cover the join with a circle seal. Adhere a heart-shaped charm to the center of the seal.

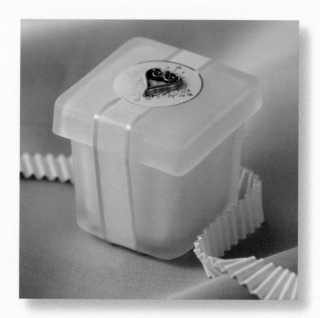

Jordon Almond Favors
by Dawn Anderson

Metal Tin Favor: Fill a round metal tin with almonds. Attach a jump ring to a metal letter. Wrap ribbon around the lid, thread one end through the jump ring, and tie in a bow.

Acrylic Box Favor: Assemble a clear acrylic box and fill with almonds. Tie ribbon around the box, inserting one end of the ribbon through the jump ring of a thank-you charm and finishing with a bow.

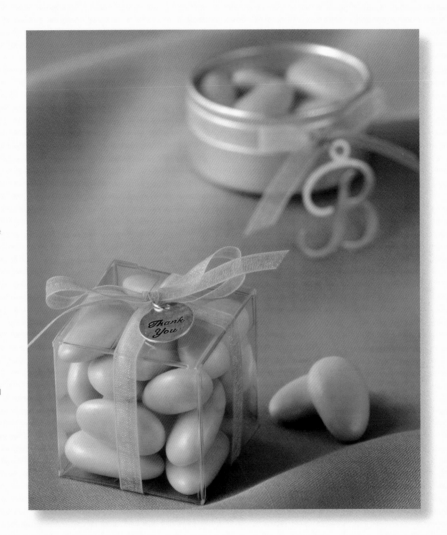

Housewarming *Party*

Use paintbrushes and paint chips to "build" one-of-a-kind party furnishings.

*P*aintbrush Invitation
by Saralyn Ewald,
Sr. Designer, Archiver's

Trim cardstock to 2¾" x 4¾" and trim the corners off one end to make a tag shape. Adhere a strip of ruler-patterned paper to the bottom edge and brush with paint. Print the invitation text onto vellum to fit in a 2¾" x 4¾" space, with a 1½" left margin. Cut the vellum to the shape of the cardstock tag. Cut the same tag shape from patterned paper. Apply rub-on letters to the painted tag to spell *HOME*. Punch a hole in the end of each tag and attach a reinforcement label to the back. Thread the tags, a small metal key, and a paintbrush onto a bead chain and secure with a fastener.

*P*aint Can Favor
by Saralyn Ewald,
Sr. Designer, Archiver's

Trim patterned paper to fit around the outside of a 16-oz. paint can and adhere in place. Cut a circle of paper to fit on top of the lid, inside the lip, and adhere in place. Tie twine around the handle of a small metal key and secure with a knot. Adhere the key to the lid of the can.

*P*aint Can Flower Holder
by Saralyn Ewald,
Sr. Designer, Archiver's

Cut a 1¼" circle template from cardstock. Cut two 3½" x 12" pieces of text paper and trace the circle template to the back of each, positioning it 1" from a long edge (upper edge) and 2½" from the adjacent edge. Cut out the circles and cut a slit from the bottom of each to the lower edge of the paper. Adhere the text papers to the top portion of a gallon-size paint can, with the circles positioned at the handles. Cut two 4" strips of key-patterned paper and adhere to the bottom portion of the can. Cut two matching strips from ruler-patterned paper and adhere to the can over the join. Trim text-patterned paper to 2¾" x 4¾" and trim the corners off one end to make a tag. Cut a matching tag from cardstock, adhere a strip of ruler-patterned paper to the bottom edge, and brush with paint. Apply rub-on letters to the painted tag to spell *HOME*. Punch a hole at the end of each tag and the paint color card strip and adhere a reinforcement label to the back of each. Using twine and ribbon, tie the tags and a metal key to the handle.

*P*otted Plant Favor
by Dawn Anderson

Cut patterned paper to fit around the outside of a cardboard pencil holder and adhere in place. Cut ribbon to fit around the container and tape the ends together where they meet. Tie lengths of ribbon through each end of a label holder and trim the tails. Print the guest's name onto cardstock, and cut out to fit behind the label holder. Bend a slight curve in the label holder to match the curve of the container. Adhere the label to the container over the ribbon ends. Insert an ivy plant into the container and arrange Spanish moss around the top.

Welcome Canvas

by Dawn Anderson

Paint the side edges of a rectangular canvas and a 1" border on the front. Dry-brush over the canvas with a lighter shade of paint. Rub paint onto a miniature metal frame and the tops of decorative brads, rubbing off the excess. Trim patterned paper to 12" x 11" and adhere to the canvas center. Cut two 5½" x 11" rectangles of patterned paper and adhere to the sides. Cover the paper joins with ribbon. Remove the prongs from the backs of the brads, and adhere the brads to each end of the ribbon. Print the text onto patterned paper, trim to size, and apply ink to the edges. Adhere the text block to patterned paper, trim ⅜" from the edges, and apply ink to the edges. Adhere the text block and attach the framed photo to the canvas. Adhere numeric stickers to square metal frames, trimming as necessary, and attach to the canvas. Wrap wire around a 1"-diameter dowel to make a double loop. Attach the wire loop to one end of a length of chain and attach the other end to a photo frame tag, using a jump ring. Tie a bow around the chain. Cut a ribbon for the hanger and adhere the ends to the back of the canvas. Hang the canvas and frame tag from a decorative drawer pull.

Baby Shower

Rich purple and teal convey the distinctive look of a designer shower.

Pacifier Invitation
by Dawn Anderson

Trim patterned paper to 4" x 4". Trim a piece of cardstock and a piece of vellum each to 4" x 5" and adhere together. Lap the layered papers over the patterned paper by ½" and adhere. Adhere ribbon over the join. Adhere the card front to ribbed paper and trim 3/16" from the edges. Adhere to cardstock and trim ½" from the edges. Tie a pacifier charm to a metal-rimmed tag with ribbon and adhere to the card. Apply rub-on lettering. Print text onto cardstock, cut to size, and adhere to the card. Attach a jelly label. Add invitation wording to the back of the card.

Toy Block Favor Box
by Dawn Anderson

Trim patterned paper to fit around the outside of a small favor box and adhere in place. Cut four pieces of ribbed paper to 1½" x 1½" and apply ink around the edges. Adhere the squares to a piece of cardstock. Trim a scant ⅛" from the edges of the squares. Adhere one square to each side of the box. Attach an alphabet letter to each side of the box.

Frosted Favor Bag
by Dawn Anderson

Cut a 1" circle from cardstock and stamp the text onto the circle. Cut a 1 3/16" circle from contrasting cardstock. Adhere the stamped circle to the contrasting circle. Install an eyelet in the top of the tag. Attach a jump ring through the eyelet and around a swirl clip. Place a small treat-filled box inside a frosted bag and turn down the top of the bag 1" twice. Attach the swirl clip to the center top of the bag. Tie ribbon in a bow around the center of the swirl clip.

Baby Rattle Invitation
by Dawn Anderson

Trim cardstock to 10½" x 7" and fold in half to make a 5¼" x 7" card. Cut a piece of patterned paper to 5¼" x 7" and adhere to the card front. Cut a 2⅛" x 7" piece of contrasting patterned paper. Sand the edges, fold in half, and adhere to the card, aligning the fold lines. Adhere two small hinges to the card. Rub a square metal frame with acrylic paint and wipe off the excess, leaving some in the grooves. Brush the top, bottom, and right edges of the card with acrylic paint. Cut patterned paper to 3½" x 1" and fold in half to make a 1¾" x 1" tag. Stamp the text onto the tag, install an eyelet on the left side, and tie several strands of metallic thread through it. Adhere the tag to the card, securing the back half to the inside. Attach the metal frame. Tie ribbon to a rattle charm and adhere to the card. Back a jelly label with patterned paper and attach to the card.

Take-Out-Box Favor
by Dawn Anderson

Print text onto patterned paper. Trim to 1¼" x 1¾", centering the text near the bottom, and trim off the corners at the top to make a tag shape. Sand the edges of the tag. Adhere to contrasting patterned paper, trim ¼" from the edges, and sand the edges of the border paper. Install an eyelet at the top of the tag and place a Washer Word over it. Thread cording through both and tie the tag to the handle of a colored take-out container. Tie ribbon in a bow around the handle.

Rattle Place Card Favor
by Dawn Anderson

Cut cardstock to 4⅛" x 7⅛" and score a line ½" from one short end for the card front. Cut another piece of cardstock to 4⅛" x 8½" and score lines 6⅝" and 8" from one short end for the card back and bottom. Trim patterned paper to 4⅛" x 6⅝", sand the edges, and adhere to the card front below the scored line. Trim patterned paper for the top to 3½" x 5", apply ink to the edges, and adhere, leaving an even border. Print the guest's name onto patterned paper for the bottom, trim to 3½" x 1", and adhere, leaving an even border. Rub paint onto the rim of the lid of a metal tin, and wipe off the excess. Dry-brush paint over narrow ribbon. Make a loop in one end of a 10" length of wire with round-nose pliers. Wrap the wire around the loop to make a coil ¾" in diameter. Pound the wire with a hammer on a hard surface to flatten it and make the rattle handle, referring to the template on page 78. Lightly adhere the filled tin to the card. Tie a bow around the handle. Position the handle under the tin so that the coil lies centered on the join between the papers. Trim the excess wire, and secure the handle and tin in place. Insert the narrow ribbon through the coil of the handle and adhere to the card along the paper join. Add text to a miniature tag and apply ink to the edges. Pin the tag to the ribbon. Attach the card front to the card back and bottom, overlapping the front card flap to the back and adhering the bottom flap to the inside of the card front.

Anniversary *Party*

Highlight the history of a happy couple with an antique-inspired color palette.

*M*ini Photo Album Invitation
by Genevieve A. Sterbenz

Unfold an accordion card. Remove the small die-cut frame and rose bouquet from the die-cut sheet. Using the frame as a template, enlarge the window opening in the card and then attach the frame and rose bouquet to the card. Tape a photo to the back of the window opening, and then secure the first panel of the card to the second panel to cover the back of the photo. Attach photos to two more die-cut frames, and adhere them to the fourth and sixth panels of the card. (Note: The first panel is adhered to the back of the second panel.) Write dates on charm tags and adhere them to the card. Print two text blocks onto vellum, keeping the text within a 4" x 5½" area. Trim two pieces of striped paper to the same size as the vellum text blocks. Layer the vellum and striped papers and adhere them with brads to the third and fifth panels of the card.

*D*ecorative Favor Box
by Genevieve A. Sterbenz

Using the box template listed on page 75, trace the template onto the wrong side of patterned paper. Cut on the marked lines and marked slot. Using the template as a guide, fold along all the indicated lines. Apply glue to the right side of tabs A, B, C, and D and adhere to the inside of the box. Place a favor in the box and close the lid. Tie ribbon around the box. Attach a name tag to the ribbon with cording.

*F*ramed Place Card
by Genevieve A. Sterbenz

Trim cardstock to fit inside the opening of an attractive frame. Cut ⅜" strips from a sticker sheet. Use the strips to create a border around the cardstock rectangle, applying strips to the top and bottom first, and then to the sides. Apply alphabet stickers to spell out the guest's name. Insert the place card in the frame.

Thank-You Card and Envelope Liner
by Genevieve A. Sterbenz

Adhere a decorative border sticker across a note card. Apply alphabet stickers to spell *thank you* above the border sticker. Place an opened envelope on the wrong side of patterned paper and trace around the outside of the envelope with a pencil. Trim away 1/16" all around. Insert the liner into the envelope, patterned side up. Fold over and crease the right and left edges of the flap to expose the gummed area of the envelope. Trim away the excess paper on the crease lines. Apply rubber cement to the wrong side of the liner flap and press to adhere to the envelope flap.

Anniversary Candle Centerpiece
by Saralyn Ewald, Sr. Designer, Archiver's

Trim patterned paper to fit around the outside of a glass candle holder, beneath the rim, overlapping pieces as necessary. Adhere in place. Fill the candle holder to the rim with floral foam. Position a pillar candle in the center, on top of the foam, and cover any visible foam with moss. Paint wood numbers corresponding to the anniversary being celebrated. Apply color from a gold leafing pen to a soft cloth and rub the cloth over the numbers to add highlights. Adhere a 5½" length of wire to the back of each number, using hot glue. Insert the numbers into the floral foam in front of the candle. Tie ribbon around the top edge of the candle holder.

Anniversary Cone Favor

by Saralyn Ewald, Sr. Designer, Archiver's

Create a collage of photos and copy them onto heavyweight paper using a color photocopier. Using the cone favor pattern on page 78, cut one piece from patterned paper and one piece from photo-collage paper. Adhere the papers, wrong sides together, with liquid glue and let dry. Roll the paper into a cone shape and secure the ends together with tacky tape. Punch holes on opposite sides of the cone about ½" from the upper edge. Make a loop at one end of a 14" length of wire with round-nose pliers and wrap the wire around the loop to make a coil ⅝" in diameter. Insert the wire into one of the punched holes from the outside. Add beads to the wire until they are 2" from the end. Insert the end into the remaining hole and make a coil at that end. Insert a thread through the top of a small tassel and insert the thread tails through a bead. Insert the thread tails into the tip of the cone and tape to the inside.

Retirement *Party*

*R*etirement Invitation
by Dawn Anderson

Trim two pieces of cardstock to 5½" x 6¾". Butt the 5½" ends together and tape along the seam to make a hinge. Trim patterned paper to 5½" x 5", fold in half to make a 5½" x 2½" hinge cover, and adhere to the card, aligning the fold with the hinge. Adhere ribbon to the lower edge of the patterned paper. Attach a woven label. Punch a ¼" hole in cardstock and adhere the punched-out circle to the center of a flat silver tag. Write text on the tag, tie cording through the loop, and secure it to the card. Print text onto patterned paper. Center and adhere a Page Pebble over the text, trim around the edges, and adhere it to the card. Spell out the remainder of the message with alphabet stickers.

*P*otted-Bulb Favor
by Dawn Anderson

Pot a flower bulb in pebbles within a copper planter. Cut a 12" length of copper wire, using a wire cutter. Make a loop using the round-nose pliers. Wrap the wire around the loop several times to make a coil ¾" in diameter. Print the guest's name onto cardstock and trim to size, allowing ½" on the left edge. Adhere the name to patterned paper and trim ⅛" from the edges. Apply paint to a decorative copper brad and wipe off the excess. Insert the brad into the end of the tag. Tie sisal twine around the brad, knot the ends, and hang from the wire coil. Insert the wire stem under the coil into the pot, cutting it to the desired height.

*H*appy Retirement Canvas
by Dawn Anderson

Paint a rectangular canvas. Print text onto patterned paper. Trim each word to 9¾" x 3". Adhere the words to contrasting patterned paper and trim ¼" from the edges. Trim a third patterned paper to 12" x 11". Adhere the word blocks to the third paper. Secure photo anchors in place with circle brads along the top and bottom edges of the word blocks. Adhere the message to the canvas. Adhere ribbon over the side edges of the paper. Rub the decorative brads with paint, wiping off the excess. Remove the backs from the brads and adhere the brad tops over the ends of the ribbon.

Please join us...

Event	*Retirement Party*
Date	*March 12, 2006*
Time	*7:00 pm*
Place	*Bandana Square*
	St. Paul, Minnesota
RSVP	*By March 5, 2006*

*P*lease Join Us . . .
Retirement Invitation
by Christine Falk and Livia McRee

Scan a scenic beach photo into a computer and size the image to 7" x 5". Print the photo onto cardstock and cut out. Print the invitation text onto vellum to fit within a 7" x 6" space, allowing for 1" at the top to be folded over. Trim to size. Tear a corner piece from patterned paper and adhere to the lower-right corner of the vellum, aligning edges. Fold 1" of the vellum to the back side at the top. Slip the vellum over the photo, aligning the edges. Install an eyelet 2" from both side edges, ½" from the top. Insert raffia through the eyelets and tie a bow. Glue two miniature starfish to the card.

*B*ath Salts Favor
by Christine Falk and Livia McRee

Fill a glass bottle with bath salts and secure with a cork. Adhere a die-cut tag to cardstock and trim ⅛" from the edges. Write the guest's name on the tag and attach a miniature starfish. Punch a hole at the end of the tag and wrap a small piece of raffia ribbon through the hole, knotting the ends together. Wrap a few strands of raffia ribbon around the neck of the bottle and slip the tag onto the ribbon on one side. Tie the ribbon tails together in a knot.

*V*ellum Candle Wraps
by Christine Falk and Livia McRee

Scan two beach photos into a computer and size the images to 12" x 8". Print each onto vellum, and trim the vellum sheets to the height of two glass candle holders. Place the vellum around the candle holder and trim away the excess, allowing ½" for the overlap. Apply rub-on letters. Secure the vellum to the candle holders with spray adhesive. Secure the vellum edges with tape.

Project Materials

New Year's Party Invitation
by Saralyn Ewald

Pg. 6

Cardstock

Metallic paper: Paper Adventures

Patterned paper: Creative Imaginations

Shimmer paper: The Paper Company

Clock charm

Font: Hoefler, Johnathan Hoefler Type Foundry

Celebrate Coaster
by Saralyn Ewald

Pg. 6

4³⁄₈" diameter glass coaster or candle holder with lip

Metallic paper, two colors: Paper Adventures

Shimmer paper: The Paper Company

Alphabet stamps: PSX

Ink: StazOn, Tsukineko

Clock charm: Impress

Flexible liquid glue: Lineco

Paper Glaze: Aleene's

Star paper punch: Fiskars

New Year's Party Crackers
by Saralyn Ewald

Pg. 6

Heavy cardstock

Patterned paper: Creative Imaginations

Mulberry paper, 12" squares

Scalloped note cards: Memory Box

Party cracker snaps: Impress

Filling for snaps

Wine Glass Charm
by Saralyn Ewald

Pg. 8

1¼" earring hoop: Westrim Crafts

Crimping bead: Westrim Crafts

Assorted beads: Bead Heaven

Celestial charm: Bead Heaven

Jump ring

Chain-nose pliers

Ice Bucket
by Saralyn Ewald

Pg. 8

Metal planter with claw feet

Patterned paper: Creative Imaginations

Flexible liquid glue: Lineco

Mod Podge: Plaid

Party Hat
by Dawn Anderson

Pg. 9

Cardstock

Mulberry paper

Patterned paper, two-sided: American Traditional Designs

⅛" eyelets, metal-rimmed tag, and Page Pebble: Making Memories

Circle sticker: Marah Johnson, Creative Imaginations

Elastic cording

Font: Times New Roman, Microsoft

Double-sided tacky tape

Eyelet setting tool and hammer

Sewing machine

Valentine Party Invitation
by Saralyn Ewald

Pg. 10

Cardstock

Patterned paper: Creative Imaginations; Autumn Leaves; The Paper Company

18-karat gold leafing pen: Krylon

3 small ivory buttons: La Mode

Metallic fiber: On The Surface

Decorative Charger Plate
by Saralyn Ewald

Pg. 10

13" charger with 2¾" rim

Patterned paper: Creative Imaginations; Autumn Leaves; The Paper Company

18-karat gold leafing pen: Krylon

Flexible liquid glue: Lineco

Matte Mod Podge: Plaid

Pinstripe Favor Box
by Dawn Anderson

Pg. 10

2" x 2" x 2" pinstripe favor box: Wedding Things

Cardstock

Ribbon: Midori

Coin mount: Nunn Design

Page Pebble and jump rings: Making Memories

Heart Soap Favor
by Dawn Anderson

Pg. 12

3½" x 2½" x 1½" slider box

Cardstock

Patterned paper: Sonnets, Creative Imaginations

Ribbon: Mokuba

Poemstone: Sonnets, Creative Imaginations

Thank-you tag: Hirschberg Schutz & Company Inc.

Lacy heart charm

Heart soap

Tissue paper

Valentine Cone Favor
by Saralyn Ewald

Pg. 13

Cardstock

Patterned paper: Autumn Leaves

18-karat gold leafing pen: Krylon

4 small ivory buttons: La Mode

Metallic fiber: On The Surface

Wire-edged ribbon

Flexible Liquid Glue: Lineco

Double-sided dry tacky tape: Suze Weinberg's Wondertape

¼" hole punch

Heart Charm Invitation
by Dawn Anderson

Pg. 13

Cardstock

Patterned paper: Autumn Leaves; Bo-Bunny Press; Scrapworks

Ribbon and spiral clip: Making Memories

Heart charm

Size 6 seed bead

20-gauge spool wire

Font: Papyrus and Viner Hand ITC, Microsoft

Round-nose and chain-nose pliers

Wire cutter

Easter Invitation
by Dawn Anderson

Pg. 14

Cardstock: ColorMates

Patterned paper: PSX; Sonnets, Creative Imaginations

Trim: Mokuba

Page tab: Nunn Design

Metal art tag: K & Company

Ribbon

Glitter glue pen

Sequins: Cartwright's Sequins

Bunny image: *Treasury of Animal Illustrations from Eighteenth-Century Sources,* Dover

Fonts: Monotype Corsiva and Viner Hand ITC, Microsoft

Easter Basket Favor
by Dawn Anderson

Pg. 14

Oval papier-mâché box

Cardstock

Patterned paper: Sonnets, Creative Imaginations

Acrylic paint: Americana, DecoArt

Trim: Mokuba

Ribbon

Eyelet and Charmed Word: Making Memories

Glitter glue pen

Bunny image: *Treasure of Animal Illustrations from Eighteenth-Century Sources,* Dover

Fonts: Viner Hand ITC, Microsoft

Glittered Egg Vase
by Dawn Anderson

Pg. 14

6" papier-mâché egg

1⅞" Country Candle Cup: Darice

4" wood disk

X-Acto knife

Water-based sealer: Delta

Acrylic paint and Glamour Dust: DecoArt

Matte varnish

Dries clear adhesive: The Art Glittering System

Cardstock

Font: Monotype Corsiva, Microsoft

Floral clay: Flora Craft

Wood glue

Glass vase

Easter Egg Place Cards
by Dave Brethauer

Pg. 16

Note cards: Memory Box

Cardstock

Polka-dot ribbon, 1½" wide

Ribbon, ⅛" wide

1" egg punch: Carla Craft

Font: AL Constitution, Autumn Leaves

Chocolate Bunny Favor

by Dawn Anderson

Pg. 17

Cellophane bag

Patterned paper: Paper Adventures

1/8" eyelet, metal rimmed tag, and ribbon: Making Memories

Chipboard alphabet letter: Li'l Davis Designs

Font: Times New Roman, Microsoft

Stapler and staples

Circle cutter: Fiskars

Chocolate bunny: Bissinger's

Egg candy

Shredded paper Easter grass

Flag Invitation

by Genevieve A. Sterbenz

Pg. 18

4½" x 6½" tags

Warren Kimble flags: Wallies

Cardstock

Jolee's by You PTR Banner of Flags: EK Success

You're Invited rubber stamp: Wordsworth

Ink

Embossing powder

Ribbon

Star hole punch: Paper Shapers

Heat tool

Star Luminary

by Genevieve A. Sterbenz

Pg. 18

Patterned paper

Textured cardstock

Warren Kimble flags: Wallies

Luminary template: Déjà Views Lil' Pop 'n View Templates (Celebration Set): C-Thru Ruler

Votive holder and tea light (Be sure to choose a votive holder that will prevent the flame from reaching the paper.)

Flag Garland

by Genevieve A. Sterbenz

Pg. 18

(for a 1-yard-long garland)

Textured cardstock

Warren Kimble flags: Wallies

Star from luminary template: Déjà Views Lil' Pop 'n View Templates (Celebration Set): C-Thru Ruler

Narrow gold cording

Spray adhesive

Fourth of July Favor Basket

by Dawn Anderson

Pg. 20

Nut-cup basket: D. Blümchen & Company

Cardstock

Cording, 1/8" eyelet, mesh star eyelet and ribbon: Making Memories

Font: AL Any Time, Autumn Leaves

Seed-Packet Favor

by Dawn Anderson

Pg. 20

Cardstock

Patterned paper

Flag seed packet: American Meadows

Brad: Scrap Arts

Ribbon

Font: AL Any Time, Autumn Leaves

1/8" hole punch

Pinwheel

by Genevieve A. Sterbenz

Pg. 21

Cardstock

Solid paper

Patterned paper

Pushpin

Seed beads

12"-long wood dowel, 1/4" in diameter

Spray adhesive

Star hole punch: Paper Shapers

Block of Styrofoam

Halloween Party Invitation

by Dawn Anderson

Pg. 22

Cardstock

Patterned paper: Bo-Bunny Press; 7gypsies; Scrapworks

Ribbon

Negative strip: Narratives by Karen Russell, Creative Imaginations

Alphabet stickers: Karen Foster Design

Brads and photo anchors: Making Memories

Font: AL Any Time font, Autumn Leaves

Skeleton Thank-You Card
by Dawn Anderson

Pg. 22

Cardstock

Patterned paper: 7gypsies; Scrapworks

Ribbon: Making Memories

Negative strip: Narratives by Karen Russell, Creative Imaginations

Alphabet stickers: Karen Foster Design

Skeleton charm

Halloween Pinwheel
by Genevieve A. Sterbenz

Pg. 23

Glossy solid paper

Patterned paper

Textured paper

Pushpin

Acrylic paint

Seed beads

12"-long wood dowel, 1/4" in diameter

Round hole punch: Paper Shapers

Spray adhesive

Block of Styrofoam

Halloween Favor Basket
by Dawn Anderson

Pg. 24

Nut-cup basket: D. Blümchen & Company

Cardstock

Patterned paper

Bat button: Susan Clarke Originals

Font: Tempo Grunge, Microsoft

Wine Glass Charms
by Dawn Anderson

Pg. 24

Assorted small beads

Halloween charm with loop

Jump ring: Making Memories

24-gauge wire

Chain-nose pliers

Round-nose pliers

Wire cutter

Popcorn Box
by Dawn Anderson

Pg. 25

Popcorn box: Party Partners

Patterned paper: Bo-Bunny Press

Metal-rimmed circle tag: Making Memories

Chipboard word: Li'l Davis Designs

Ribbon

Thanksgiving Invitation
by Christine Falk

Pg. 26

Cardstock

Metallic paper

Parchment cardstock: The Paper Company

Patterned vellum: Liz King

Skeleton leaf: Black Ink Decorative Accents

2-ply gold thread: On The Surface

Size 11 glass seed beads

Fonts: Arial and Lucida Handwriting

Vellum tape

1 1/2" x 1 1/2" square punch

1 3/4" x 1 3/4" square punch

Mesh Votive Favor
by Christine Falk

Pg. 26

2 3/4" x 2 3/4" x 2 3/4" glass votive holder

Brass Rub 'n Buff and wire mesh (80 mesh woven): Amaco

Metallic trim

Brass frame: Fancifuls

Parchment cardstock: The Paper Company

1/4"-wide tacky tape: Provo Craft

Votive candle

Beaded Napkin Ring and Place Card
by Christine Falk

Pg. 26

Parchment cardstock: The Paper Company

24-gauge and 32-gauge beading wire

Size 11 seed beads

Brass leaf charm: Fancifuls

Spiral clip: Making Memories

Embroidery needle

Favor Box

by Dawn Anderson

Pg. 28

2" x 2" x 2" pinstripe favor box: Wedding Things

Cardstock

Ink: Ancient Page, Clearsnap

Ribbon and ribbon charm: Making Memories

Acrylic paint: Americana, DecoArt

Font: AL Updated Classic, Autumn Leaves

Leaf Invitation

by Saralyn Ewald

Pg. 28

Cardstock

Die-cut oak leaf cut from patterned paper: Making Memories

Raffia

Font: CK Fraternity, Creating Keepsakes

⅛" hole punch: Fiskars

Autumn Wreath

by Saralyn Ewald

Pg. 29

14" grapevine wreath

Die-cut leaves as follows:

45 maple leaves cut from assorted red cardstock

6 leaves cut from butter yellow cardstock (a combination of small and large oak)

8 leaves from orange patterned paper: Making Memories

8 leaves from assorted red cardstock (a combination of oak and maple)

7 leaves from green cardstock (a combination of oak and pointed leaves)

5 leaves from green patterned paper (a combination of oak and pointed leaves): Making Memories

High-heat glue sticks and hot glue gun

Tree Invitation

by Dave Brethauer

Pg. 31

Cardstock, note card, patterned paper, tall pine tree stamp, tall triangle stamp: Memory Box

Ink: VersaColor and VersaMagic, Tsukineko

Clear glitter glue

Clear glitter

Chocolate Bar Favor

by Dave Brethauer

Pg. 30

Slim tag, small triangle stamp, and small pine tree stamp: Memory Box

Cardstock

Ink: VersaColor and VersaMagic, Tsukineko; ColorBox, Clearsnap

Wrapped chocolate bar

Ornament Place Cards

by Dave Brethauer

Pg. 30

Note cards: Memory Box

Cardstock

Polka-dot ribbon, 1½" wide

Cording

1¼" circle punch

Font: AL Constitution, Autumn Leaves

Snowflake Thank-You Card

by Savvy Stamps

Pg. 32

3½" x 5" note card, small curly thank-you stamp, small ornate snowflake stamp, solid circle stamp: Savvy Stamps

Ribbon: May Arts

Metal-rimmed tag: American Tag

Ink: ColorBox, Clearsnap; VersaColor, Tsukineko

Glittered Pinecone Boxes

by Dawn Anderson

Pg. 33

Papier-mâché pinecone boxes: D. Blümchen & Company

Acrylic paint: Delta Ceramcoat

Dries Clear Adhesive: The Art Glittering System

Glamour Dust: DecoArt

Happy Holidays mini tags: Making Memories

Birthday Invitation
by Savvy Stamps

Pg. 34

Cardstock

Large wide-stripe circle stamp and outline-swirl cake stamp: Savvy Stamps

Ink: ColorBox, Clearsnap; VersaColor, Tsukineko

Ribbon: May Arts

Clear glitter

Rubber cement

Font: Copperplate, Microsoft

⅛" hole punch

Favor Packet
by Savvy Stamps

Pg. 34

Cardstock

Small solid circle stamp and solid circle block stamp: Savvy Stamps

Ink: ColorBox, Clearsnap

Ribbon: May Arts

Font: Copperplate, Microsoft

Treats to fill packet

Sewing machine

Cake Thank-You Card
by Savvy Stamps

Pg. 34

3½" x 5" note card, "many thanks" stamp, paper flower, small cake-slice stamp, and solid circle block stamp: Savvy Stamps

Metal-rimmed tag: American tag

Ink: ColorBox, Clearsnap; VersaColor, Tsukineko

Ribbon: May Arts

Birthday Invitation
by Dawn Anderson

Pg. 36

Cardstock

Patterned paper: Bo-Bunny Press

Striped vellum: Chatterbox

Ribbon: Morex

Snap: Making Memories

Curly tulip stamp: Savvy Stamps

Ink pens: Marvy; Tombow

Dries Clear Adhesive: The Art Glittering System

Glamour Dust: DecoArt

Font: Comic Sans MS, Microsoft

⅛" hole punch

Favor Gift Box
by Dawn Anderson

Pg. 36

2¼" x 3" x 1" box: Wedding Things

Cardstock

Fabric letter: Scrapworks

Ribbon

Frosted Favor Bag
by Dawn Anderson

Pg. 37

7" x 3½" x 1¾" frosted bag: Jena Richards

Cardstock

Ribbon

Narrow cording

Metal art tag: K & Company

Font: Monotype Corsiva, Microsoft

Candy or other treats

Graduation Invitation
by Saralyn Ewald

Pg. 38

Patterned paper: Die Cuts with a View

20-gauge wire: Wild Wire

Rub-ons: Making Memories

Ink: Clearsnap

Font: CK Journaling, Creating Keepsakes

Pop-up glue dots: Glue Dots International

Round-nose pliers

Wire Photo Holder Favor and Thank-You Note
by Saralyn Ewald

Pg. 38

Cardstock

Patterned paper: Die Cuts with a View

20-gauge wire: Wild Wire

Ink: VersaColor, Tsukineko

Font: CK Journaling, Creating Keepsakes

Round-nose pliers

Floral Centerpiece with Photos
by Saralyn Ewald

Pg. 38

Vase

20-gauge wire: Wild Wire

Round-nose pliers

Graduation Favor Bag
by Saralyn Ewald

Pg. 40

Cellophane treat bag

Cardstock

Thank-you stamp: Hero Arts

Ink

Curling ribbon

1/8" brad

1/8" hole punch: Fiskars

Paper crimper: Fiskars

Candy

Favor Tin
by Dawn Anderson

Pg. 41

Round metal tin

Cardstock

Patterned paper: Cloud 9 Design

Ribbon: Making Memories

Small metal frame

Font: AL Updated Classic, Autumn Leaves; Times New Roman, Microsoft

Circle cutter: Fiskars

Flower Invitation
by Saralyn Ewald

Pg. 42

Cardstock: DMD

Patterned paper: Creative Imaginations

Alphabet stamps: Hero Arts

Ink: ColorBox, Clearsnap

Acrylic paint, decorative metal brad, and pink daisy: Making Memories

Font: CK Higgins Handprint, Creating Keepsakes

1/8" hole punch

Favor Bag
by Saralyn Ewald

Pg. 42

4 1/4" x 5 1/4" glassine envelope

Cardstock: DMD

Patterned paper: Creative Imaginations

Alphabet stamps: Hero Arts

Ink: ColorBox, Clearsnap

Acrylic paint, decorative metal brad, and pink daisy: Making Memories

Font: CK Higgins Handprint, Creating Keepsakes

Pop Dots: All Night Media

1/8" hole punch

Jordon almonds

Utensil Bucket
by Saralyn Ewald

Pg. 42

Galvanized metal bucket: Ikea

Patterned paper: Creative Imaginations

Acrylic paint, decorative metal brads, and pink daisies: Making Memories

Flexible liquid glue: Lineco

Matte Mod Podge: Plaid

1/8" hole punch

Bridal Shower Invitation
by Dawn Anderson

Pg. 44

Cardstock

Patterned paper: 7gypsies

Textured cardstock: Bazzill

Dress stamp: My Sentiments Exactly

Text stamp

Metal hanger, paper flower: Savvy Stamps

Ink: Ancient Page, Clearsnap; Tombow

Cording and swirl clip: Making Memories

Dries Clear Adhesive: The Art Glittering System

Glamour Dust: DecoArt

Sequins: Cartwright's Sequins

Potpourri Favor Box
by Dawn Anderson

Pg. 44

Round acrylic box

Cardstock

Metal art label: K & Company

Ribbon

Sticker

Font: Monotype Corsiva, Microsoft

Potpourri beads

Purse Favor

by Dawn Anderson

Pg. 45

3" x 3" x 2" clear vinyl purse with metal frame: Beaucoup

Cardstock

Textured cardstock: Bazzill

Double-faced satin ribbon: Midori

Velvet flowers

Font: Monotype Corsiva, Microsoft

Mints: Wedding Things

Wedding Invitation

by Saralyn Ewald

Pg. 46

Cardstock

Patterned paper, pom-pom punch, and daisy punch: EK Success

Ribbed paper: Mrs. Grossman's

Vellum

Crystal rhinestones: Westrim Crafts

Font: Hoefler, Jonathan Hoefler Type Foundry

Vellum tape

Flower-Seed Favor

by Saralyn Ewald

Pg. 46

Packet of flower seeds

Cardstock

Patterned paper, pom-pom punch, and daisy punch: EK Success

Ribbed paper: Mrs. Grossman's

Vellum

Font: Hoefler, Jonathan Hoefler Type Foundry

Vellum tape

¼" hole punch

Candle Decoration

by Saralyn Ewald

Pg. 46

6¾" square papier-mâché box

Patterned paper: EK Success

4" tall wooden letters to spell "LOVE"

Acrylic paint: Plaid

Floral foam blocks and sheet moss: FloraCraft

Flexible liquid glue: Lineco

Hot glue gun and glue sticks

Three 3" x 6" pillar candles

Three glass candle holders

Two artificial roses with buds

Cake stand: Williams Sonoma

Wedding Rings Invitation

by Christine Falk

Pg. 48

Cardstock

Metallic paper

Patterned vellum: The Paper Company

Ribbon

Craft wedding rings: Modern Romance "Favor-It"

Vellum tape: 3M

Fonts: Arial and Edwardian Script ITC

1½" x 1½" square punch: Stampin' Up

1¾" x 1¾" square punch: Marvy Uchida

Candle Favor

by Dawn Anderson

Pg. 48

Frosted glass candle box with lid: Wrap with Us

Ribbon: Mokuba

Circle seal sticker: Mrs. Grossman's

Charm: Making Memories

Jordon Almond Favors

by Dawn Anderson

Pg. 49

METAL TIN FAVOR

2" diameter metal tin with clear lid

Ribbon: Offray

Metal alphabet letter and jump ring: Making Memories

Jordon almonds

Pg. 49

ACRYLIC BOX FAVOR

1½" x 1½" x 1½" clear acrylic box

Ribbon: Offray

Thank-you charm: Hirschberg Schutz & Company Inc.

Jordon almonds

Paintbrush Invitation
by Saralyn Ewald

Pg. 50

Small paintbrush with a hole at the end of the handle

Cardstock

Patterned paper: 7gypsies

Vellum

6" of bead chain with fastener: Darice

Small metal key: K & Company

Acrylic paint and rub-ons: Making Memories

Clear reinforcement labels: Avery

Font: CK Typist, Creating Keepsakes

1/4" hole punch

Paint Can Favor
by Saralyn Ewald

Pg. 50

16-oz. paint can with lid: The Container Store

Patterned paper: Pickle Press

Metal key: K & Company

Twine

Paint Can Flower Holder
by Saralyn Ewald

Pg. 50

Gallon-size paint can with handle

Cardstock

Patterned paper: K & Company; Pickle Press; 7gypsies

Paint color card strip

Metal key: K & Company

Twine

Ribbon

Acrylic paint and rub-ons: Making Memories

Clear reinforcement labels: Avery

1/4" hole punch

Potted Plant Favor
by Dawn Anderson

Pg. 52

Cardboard pencil holder with metal base

Cardstock

Patterned paper: Basic Grey

Label holder: Making Memories

Ribbon

Font: Monotype Corsiva, Microsoft

Ivy plant in a plastic pot

Spanish moss

Welcome Canvas
by Dawn Anderson

Pg. 53

24" x 12" canvas: Canvas Concepts

Acrylic paint: Americana, DecoArt

Patterned paper: Déjà Views

Ribbon

Miniature decorative metal frame

Decorative square brads and jump ring: Making Memories

Square metal frames: Li'l Davis Designs

Numeric stickers: EK Success

Ink: Ancient Page, Clearsnap

Photo frame tag: Nunn Design

2" length of chain

16-gauge wire

Font: Monotype Corsiva, Microsoft

1"-diameter dowel

Decorative drawer pull

Pacifier Invitation
by Dawn Anderson

Pg. 54

Cardstock

Patterned paper: Paper Inc.

Patterned vellum: The Paper Company

Ribbed paper: Mrs. Grossman's

Ribbon

Jelly label, metal-rimmed tag, rub-ons: Making Memories

Pacifier charm: Downtown Crafts

Font: Papyrus, Microsoft

Vellum adhesive: 3M

Toy Block Favor Box
by Dawn Anderson

Pg. 54

2" x 2" x 2" box: Sophie's Favors

Cardstock

Patterned paper: Creative Imaginations

Ribbed paper: Mrs. Grossman's

Alphabet letters: K & Company

Ink pen: Marvy

Frosted Favor Bag
by Dawn Anderson

Pg. 54

7" x 3½" x 1¾" frosted bag: Jena Richards

2⅝" x 1⁵⁄₁₆" x 1¼" ballotin box: Sophie's Favors

Cardstock

Eyelet, jump ring, and swirl clip: Making Memories

Stamp: Savvy Stamps

Ink pen: Marvy

Ribbon

Circle cutter: Fiskars

Baby Rattle Invitation
by Dawn Anderson

Pg. 56

Cardstock

Patterned paper: Carolee's Creations

⅛" eyelet, hinges, jelly label: Making Memories

Rattle charm: Westrim Crafts

Square metal frame: Marcella by Kay

Ribbon

Metallic thread: DMC

Baby and shower stamps: Savvy Stamps

Ink: Memories, Stewart Superior Corporation

Acrylic paint: Delta Ceramcoat

Take-Out-Box Favor
by Dawn Anderson

Pg. 56

Colored take-out box

Patterned paper: Carolee's Creations; Baby Scrapbook Paper Collection, Vintage Scrappy Chic

Ribbon

Cording, ⅛" eyelet, and Washer Words: Making Memories

Font: AL Any Time, Autumn Leaves

Rattle Place Card Favor
by Dawn Anderson

Pg. 57

Heavy cardstock

Patterned paper: Carolee's Creations; Baby Scrapbook Paper Collection, Vintage Scrappy Chic

Metal tin with clear lid

16-gauge wire

Organza ribbon and narrow ribbon

Acrylic paint: Delta Ceramcoat

Ink: Ancient Page, Clearsnap

Safety pin: Li'l Davis Designs

Miniature tag: DMD

Font: AL Any Time, Autumn Leaves

Round-nose pliers

Wire cutter

Mints

Mini Photo Album Invitation
by Genevieve A. Sterbenz

Pg. 58

Déjà Views Tid Bits Story Book: C-Thru Ruler

Striped paper: Anna Griffin

Vellum

Die-cut frames and scrapbook accessories in blue roses: Anna Griffin

Eyelet charm tags, circle brads: Making Memories

Marker

Font: Nuptial Script, Microsoft

Decorative Favor Box
by Genevieve A. Sterbenz

Pg. 58

Patterned paper: Anna Griffin

Déjà Views Take-Out Food Box Template: C-Thru Ruler

Ribbon

Eyelet charm tag: Making Memories

Marker

Cording

Framed Place Card
by Genevieve A. Sterbenz

Pg. 58

Small frame

Cardstock

Alphabet and border stickers: Anna Griffin

Thank-You Card and Envelope Liner
by Genevieve A. Sterbenz

Pg. 60

THANK-YOU CARD

6¼" x 4¼" note card

Border sticker: Anna Griffin

Alphabet stickers: Anna Griffin

ENVELOPE LINER

Envelope for a 6¼" x 4¼" note card

Patterned paper: Anna Griffin

Rubber cement

Anniversary Candle Centerpiece
by Saralyn Ewald

Pg. 60

3" x 6" pillar candle

Glass candle holder, 5½" wide x 6¾" tall

Patterned paper

Ribbon

4"-tall wood numbers

Acrylic paint: Making Memories

18-karat gold leafing pen: Krylon

16-gauge wire

Floral foam blocks

Sheet moss: FloraCraft

Hot glue gun and glue sticks

Anniversary Cone Favor
by Saralyn Ewald

Pg. 61

Heavyweight paper

Patterned paper

20-gauge wire: Wild Wire

Glass beads

Small tassel

Thread

Flexible liquid glue: Lineco

Double-sided dry tacky tape: Suze Weinberg's Wondertape

Round-nose pliers

Wire cutter

⅛" hole punch

Retirement Invitation
by Dawn Anderson

Pg. 62

Cardstock

Patterned paper: Bo-Bunny Press

Ribbon

Woven label, oval Page Pebble, cording: Making Memories

Small, flat silver tag: Nunn Design

Alphabet stickers: Marcella by Kay

Pen: Zig Millenium

Font: Papyrus, Microsoft

¼" hole punch

Potted-Bulb Favor
by Dawn Anderson

Pg. 62

Narcissus bulb, copper planter, and pebbles: Smith & Hawkin

Cardstock

Patterned paper: Bo-Bunny Press

Antique copper decorative brad: Making Memories

Acrylic paint: Americana, DecoArt

Handmade sisal twine: Provo Craft

16-gauge copper wire

Font: Papyrus, Microsoft

Round-nose pliers

Wire cutter

Happy Retirement Canvas
by Dawn Anderson

Pg. 62

11" x 14" artist canvas: Fredrix

Patterned paper: Bo-Bunny Press; NRN Designs

Velvet ribbon, photo anchors, mini circle brads, antique copper decorative brads: Making Memories

Acrylic paint: Americana, DecoArt; Delta Ceramcoat

Font: Papyrus, Microsoft

Please Join Us . . . Retirement Invitation
by Christine Falk and Livia McRee

Pg. 64

Cardstock

Patterned paper: Carolee's Creations

Vellum

Beach photo

Eyelets

Raffia ribbon: DMD

Miniature starfish: Magic Scraps

Font: Banff and Times New Roman, Microsoft

Bath Salts Favor
by Christine Falk and Livia McRee

Pg. 64

Glass bottle with cork stopper

Cardstock

Die-cut tag

Raffia ribbon: DMD

Fine-tip marking pen

Miniature starfish: Magic Scraps

Bath salts

⅛" hole punch

Vellum Candle Wraps
by Christine Falk and Livia McRee

Pg. 65

Glass candle holder, 3½" diameter x 6" high

Glass candle holder, 3½" diameter x 7½" high

12" x 12" vellum sheets

Beach photos

Rub-ons: Making Memories

Vellum adhesive spray: Creative Imaginations

Vellum tape: 3M

Pillar candles to fit candle holders

Party hat pattern

Enlarge pattern 125%.

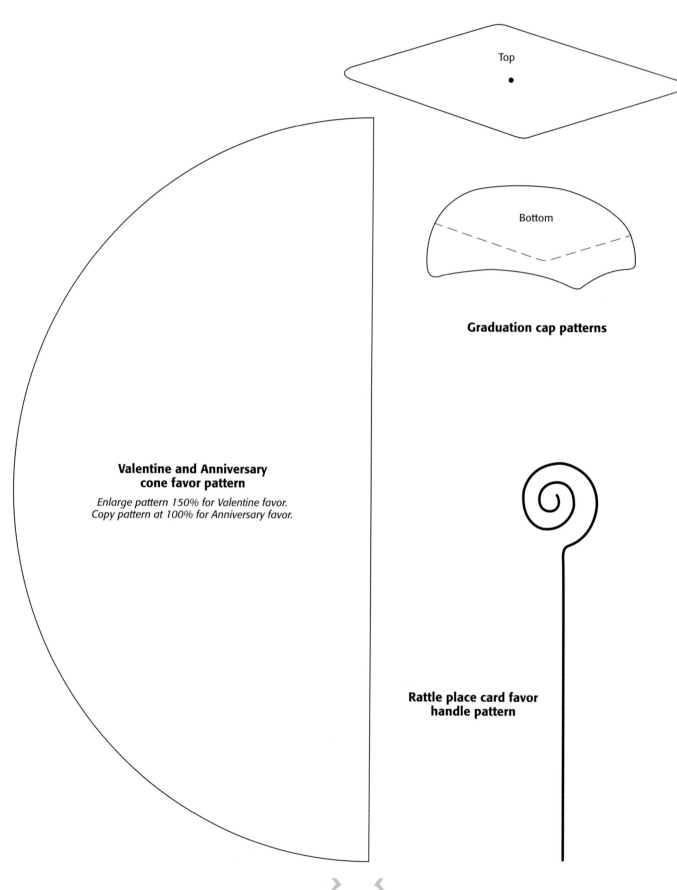

Top

Bottom

Graduation cap patterns

**Valentine and Anniversary
cone favor pattern**

*Enlarge pattern 150% for Valentine favor.
Copy pattern at 100% for Anniversary favor.*

**Rattle place card favor
handle pattern**

Resources

7gypsies
www.sevengypsies.com
Patterned paper

Archiver's Inc. – The Photo Memory Store
www.archiversonline.com

American Meadows Inc.
www.americanmeadows.com
Flower seed packets

Beaucoup
www.beau-coup.com
3" x 3" x 2" clear vinyl purse with metal frame

Bissinger's
www.bissingers.com
Chocolate bunny

Bo-Bunny Press
www.bobunny.com
Patterned paper

Cartwright's Sequins
www.ccartwright.com
Sequins

***Creating Keepsakes* Scrapbook Magazine**
www.creatingkeepsakes.com
Fonts

D. Blümchen & Company Inc.
www.blumchen.com
Nut-cup baskets, papier-mâché pinecone boxes

DecoArt Inc.
www.decoart.com
Acrylic paint

Delta Technical Coating Inc.
www.deltacrafts.com
Acrylic paint

Downtown Crafts
www.downtowncrafts.com
Pacifier charm

EK Success
www.eksuccess.com
Zig markers, Jolee's stickers

Fancifuls Inc.
www.fancifulsinc.com
Charms

Autumn Leaves
www.autumnleaves.com
Patterned paper

Glue Dots International, LLC
www.gluedots.com
Adhesive dots

Hero Arts Rubber Stamps Inc.
www.heroarts.com
Rubber stamps

Hoefler & Frere Jones
www.typography.com
Hoefler font

Loew-Cornell Inc.
www.loew-cornell.com
Paintbrushes

Impress
www.impressrubberstamps.com
Circle punch and egg-shaped punch, party cracker snaps, clock charms, stamps, papers, ink, and embellishments

Jena Richards Inc.
www.jenarichards.com
Frosted bags

Kate's Paperie
www.katespaperie.com
Cardstock; patterned, solid, and textured paper; vellum; die-cut scrapbook accessories; stickers; tags; envelopes; rubber stamps; ink; embossing powder; ribbon; star and round hole punches; brads; eyelet charm tags; adhesive

Memory Box, Inc.
www.memoryboxco.com
Note cards, cardstock, triangle stamps, pine tree stamps

Nunn Design
www.nunndesign.com
Metal embellishments

Party Partners
www.partypartnersdesign.com
Popcorn box

Savvy Stamps
www.savvystamps.com
Stamps, note cards, paper flowers, tiny metal hangers

Smith & Hawkin Ltd.
www.smithhawkin.com
Copper pot, narcissus bulb, pebbles

Sophie's Favors
www.sophiesfavors.com
2" x 2" x 2" box, ballotin box, Midori double-faced satin ribbon

Sticker Studio
www.stickerstudio.com
Patterned paper

The C-Thru Ruler Company
www.cthruruler.com
Déjà Views Tid Bits Story Book, Lil' Pop 'n View Pattern Templates (Celebration Set) and Take-Out Food Box template

Therm O Web
www.thermoweb.com
Adhesives

The McCall Pattern Company (Wallies)
www.wallies.com
Warren Kimble Flags

Wedding Things
www.weddingthings.com
Favor boxes, mints

Wrap With Us
www.wrapwithus.com
Frosted glass candle box

Contributors

A special thanks to the contributors whose products were used in this book.

7gypsies; Autumn Leaves (Foofala); Bo-Bunny Press; DecoArt Inc.; Delta Technical Coating Inc.; EK Success; Fancifuls Inc.; Glue Dots International, LLC; Hero Arts Rubber Stamps Inc.; Kate's Paperie; Loew-Cornell Inc.; Memory Box Inc.; Nunn Design; Savvy Stamps; Sticker Studio; The C-Thru Ruler Company; Therm O Web; The McCall Pattern Company (Wallies)

About the Designers

Dawn Anderson has worked in the publishing industry for 12 years, and especially enjoys the opportunity to develop craft books as an editor at Martingale & Company. She has had numerous designs published in a variety of books and magazines over the years, including *Collage Cards: 45 Great Greetings!* (Martingale & Company, 2004).

Dave Brethauer has been designing cards and paper for 10 years. He and his wife, Monica, own Memory Box Inc., a scrapbook-paper and rubber-stamp company that sells to stores across the United States. He is the author of *Stamp in Color: Techniques for Enhancing Your Artwork* (Martingale & Company, 2000), and has taught hundreds of classes covering painting and colored-pencil techniques.

Saralyn Ewald has a BFA in ceramics and loves to create art and explore different mediums—her current favorite being papercrafting. She is the senior designer at Archiver's: The Photo Memory Store, and has contributed project designs to several books, including *Collage Cards: 45 Great Greetings!* (Martingale & Company, 2004), and *Layer by Layer: Collage Projects for Home Decorating* (Martingale & Company, 2004).

Christine Falk has always had an interest in crafts and interior decorating and enjoys creating projects for publication. Her recent project designs can be found in *Layer by Layer: Collage Projects for Home Decorating* (Martingale & Company, 2004). Christine has had a 12-year career as a freelance editor, producing newsletters and working on self-published books of poetry.

Livia McRee began her creative career on the staff of *Handcraft Illustrated* magazine. From there, she began writing about and designing craft projects for book and magazine publishers, including *Paper Crafts Magazine*. She has authored books on craft topics and contributed designs to many publications.

Cindi Nelson started rubber stamping 16 years ago when she went to work for Impress Rubber Stamps while attending the University of Washington in Seattle. Five years ago she and a business partner started a rubber-stamp line called Savvy Stamps. They both have a passion for beautiful paper and classic designs. Cindi's work has appeared in a variety of publications over the years, including *Collage Cards: 45 Great Greetings!* (Martingale & Company, 2004).

Genevieve A. Sterbenz is the author of seven craft and home-decorating books. Genevieve is also a longtime contributing designer for books, magazines, and newspapers, and can frequently be seen on television presenting decorating ideas. Genevieve is the founder of Greenbean Productions, which creates custom scrapbooks, keepsake photo albums, invitations, and gift-wrap designs for private clients.